I dance because
I am rich.

—Makah Chieftain

LIBRARY OF CONGRESS CATALOGING-IN-PUBLICATION DATA
Cohlene, Terri, 1950
  Clamshell Boy / by Terri Cohlene; illustrated by Charles Reasoner.
      p. cm. — (Native American legends)
  Summary: Retells the legend of Clamshell Boy, who rescues a captured group of children from the dreaded wild woman Basket Woman. Includes information on the customs and lifestyles of the Makah Indians.
  ISBN 086593 001 5
  1. Makah Indians — Legends. 2. Makah Indians — Social life and customs — Juvenile literature.
(1. Makah Indiana — Legends. 2. Indians of North America — Legends. 3. Makah Indians — Social life and customs. 4. Indians of North America — Social life and customs.) 1. Reasoner, Charles, ill.
II. Title. III. Series.
E99.M19C67 1990
398.2 0979 — dc20   AC   CIP   89-10744

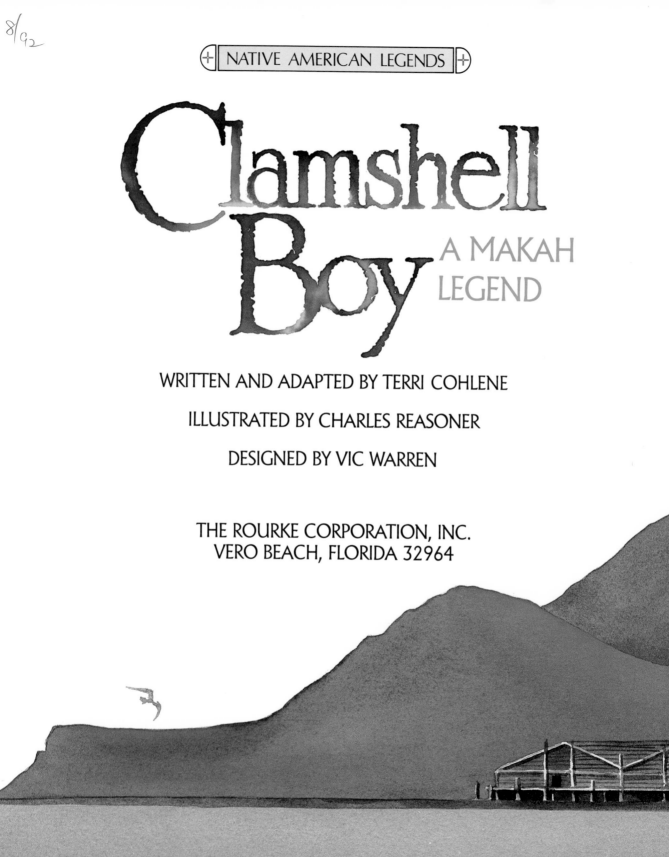

8/92

Clamshell Boy

A MAKAH LEGEND

WRITTEN AND ADAPTED BY TERRI COHLENE

ILLUSTRATED BY CHARLES REASONER

DESIGNED BY VIC WARREN

THE ROURKE CORPORATION, INC.
VERO BEACH, FLORIDA 32964

 ong ago, in the days of the ancestors, a young Makah girl named
Salmonberry was playing with her friends on the beach. It was dur-
ing the month of the sparkling moon, and each day the sun spirit
smiled longer on the People of the Cape.

The women put their clamming baskets on their backs and called to the children.
"Come! The shadows grow long. We should return to the village."

"But the sun still hovers over the water," said Salmonberry. "Please let us stay a
little longer."

Her mother squinted her dark eyes toward the horizon. "It will soon be time for
Basket Woman to wander the shore. You must be home before the sun sleeps."

"We promise," chorused the children.

When the women had gone, Salmonberry called to her friends. "Who has seen this giant, Basket Woman? I do not believe she is real. Our mothers are afraid of shadows, but not I!"

"You do not believe Basket Woman comes to the beaches at sunset?" asked one of the others. "You do not believe she scoops children up and carries them off in her basket to roast for dinner? That is what the elders tell us."

Salmonberry hopped onto a driftwood log as a wave teased her bare feet. "Let us play a hiding game until the sun sleeps. You will see. And we shall be back at our longhouse before we are missed."

Soon they were laughing at their mothers' words as they played their hiding game. Suddenly, someone pointed over Salmonberry's head. "I see Basket Woman!"

"You do not frighten me," mocked Salmonberry to her friend.

"But I see her too!" shouted another.

Salmonberry whirled around. "Basket Woman!"

6

7

Salmonberry ran to her friends and watched the giant wild woman separate from the shadows. "Who calls my name?" hissed Basket Woman. Her sunken eyes swept the beach until they rested on the huddled children.

In two steps, she was standing over them. "Were you not told of the dangers here after dark?" she croaked.

Salmonberry smelled smoke and grease in the wild woman's long tangled hair. "Y-y-yes," she stammered. "We were just returning home. Our parents are waiting."

Basket Woman nodded. "I do not wish you to be scolded. Let me help you. I can travel the distance in a few steps."

The children clung together.

Basket Woman scowled. "You have heard tales of me?" she asked.

The children nodded.

Basket Woman hung her head. "They are lies. Let me help you and thus clear my name."

Salmonberry hesitated. She thought of her empty stomach. "I believe you," she said. "I will help you clear your name."

Basket Woman grinned a black-toothed smile and lowered her basket so the girl could climb in.

"Come," called Salmonberry. "We are late. We can still be home before mealtime . . . or are you afraid?"

"We are not afraid," the children said. And one by one, they climbed into the huge basket. Basket Woman lifted it onto her back and adjusted the tumpline on her forehead.

As the giant woman strode away, Salmonberry saw treetops rushing past overhead. Something is wrong, she thought. Suddenly, her bravery vanished. "This is not the way to our village!" She cried.

Basket Woman stopped. "You are too clever," she said, laughing. As the children tried to crawl out, she shook them back down to the bottom of the basket.

"Let us go!" demanded Salmonberry. "Our brave warriors will come after you!" But before she could think of a way to escape, the wild woman's giant hand descended into the basket and covered everyone's eyes with sticky pitch.

"Now, hush!" warned Basket Woman. "Or I shall seal your mouths too. You would have done well to heed the words of your elders." She laughed as she hoisted the basket onto her back. "Soon enough, I shall be roasting you over my cookfire. I have been too long without the delicious taste of naughty children."

When the children did not come home, Salmonberry's mother went in search of them. "They will no longer be allowed to play on the beach," she muttered. "They must learn to follow rules and to hold their promise sacred."

Soon she reached the place where they had been digging clams. She could see no one. "Children!" she called. "Come out from hiding. Your game makes me angry!" The only sounds she heard were splashing waves and a seabird calling to its mate. The woman looked at the disappearing sunrays. "Am I too late?" she thought.

As a sandcrab scuttled across the beach, the woman saw a giant footprint in the sand. "Basket Woman!" she wailed. The sea was washing smooth the children's prints, but she could still see some leading to the larger impression left by the basket.

Salmonberry's mother followed the giant footprints until they entered the forest. "My daughter is lost," she moaned. "All the children are lost." She dropped to her knees by a pile of discarded shells and wept.

o one knew where Basket Woman lived. Her house was far away, perhaps deep in the forest. No one had ever tracked her, and stolen children never returned.

Tears slid from the woman's cheek and fell onto an open clamshell. There, they shimmered with life and slowly began taking form. First they took the shape of a baby, then grew into a handsome young boy. Salmonberry's mother stopped sobbing. "Who are you?" she asked in amazement.

"It is I, Clamshell Boy. You called me from the spirit of this shell. Why are you crying?" he asked.

"Basket Woman has stolen all the children. She has stolen Salmonberry, my only child. I shall never see her again, for it is well known that Basket Woman eats children."

"You are my mother," said Clamshell Boy. "For I was born of your tears. I shall help you. I shall find the children."

The woman shook her head and wept anew. "It is hopeless," she said. "No one can save them now."

They returned to the village and told The People what had happened. "My spirit is strong," said Clamshell Boy. "I shall find the children. I shall bring them home."

As the boy prepared for his quest, the chief gave him his own canoe. His mother brought pouches of dried salmon, fresh water, and dried berries mixed with whale fat. "You must have good food to keep your strength," she said.

Clamshell Boy set off on his journey. He paddled a great distance along the coast until he arrived at a place where a forested bluff rose above the sea.

At daybreak, Clamshell Boy beached his canoe and scrambled up the steep, rocky path. Walking into the woods, he soon came upon a majestic cedar near a small pond. Climbing the tree as high as he could, he scanned the view.

He saw seagulls gliding on gusty currents. He saw whales blowing water far from shore. He saw white-crested mountains and thick green treetops spreading across the land, but he did not see a giant's lodge. He did not see Basket Woman.

Before he could wonder at the wispy curl of smoke he had seen in the distance, Clamshell Boy heard a sound below. He quietly inched his way onto a lower branch. There, kneeling at the pond, was a gigantic wild woman. Her long hair was twisted and tangled, and the smell of smoke and grease wafted upward. Basket Woman!

As he lay there, still and silent, Clamshell Boy suddenly realized his face was reflected in the water over Basket Woman's shoulder. She saw it too. "How handsome I am this day," she said. She put her hand on her cheek, and Clamshell Boy did the same to his. "My hair is combed, my skin unmarked, and my eyes are no longer deep in my head."

Just then, a pinecone fell, sending ripples across the reflection. Basket Woman looked up. "So it was your face in the water!" she declared. "Come down at once before I pluck you from the tree and throw you into my basket!"

When Clamshell Boy climbed down, Basket Woman glared at him with hollow eyes. "Do you think I'm ugly?" she asked.

"Oh, no," said the boy. "But, I was thinking how I could help you to become more beautiful."

"You are nothing but a child. How could you help me?"

Clamshell Boy untied the pouches from his belt. "I was once ugly," he said, "but our shaman gave me this magic. Look what wonders it has done."

Basket Woman studied his face for a moment. "If what you say is true, let me try it for myself."

Clamshell Boy opened his pouches and offered them to the giant. "Take some of this and rub it on your face," he said.

Basket Woman rubbed the berries and fat and dried fish onto her skin. "I do not feel different," she said. She looked into the pond. "I do not look different, either. Perhaps I should eat you for my dinner!"

"Of course you do not look different yet," said the boy. "You must first gaze into the sea. It is part of the charm."

Basket Woman motioned
for Clamshell Boy to go first, and followed
him to the edge of the bluff. There, she knelt down
and leaned over the cliff. "I do not see anything," she said.

"Of course you do not see anything," repeated Clamshell Boy.
"You must lean further out."

She leaned further. "I still do not see anything," she said. "I think you are
tricking me."

"Just a little further," the boy urged. "The sea is a long way down."

She leaned a little further and suddenly, the ground beneath her crumbled. Basket
Woman fell crashing to her death.

Clamshell Boy followed the path leading toward the smoke he had seen earlier. Soon, he came upon a lodge—bigger, even, than the lodge of a chief.

He peered into the smoke-filled room and saw children tied to the walls. "Is Salmonberry here?" he called. "It is I, Clamshell Boy, sent by our mother to bring you home!"

A small voice cried out, "I am Salmonberry."

Clamshell Boy untied Salmonberry and the others and helped remove the pitch from their eyes. He told them what had happened. "She cannot harm you now," he said. "Basket Woman is dead."

The children cried out in relief. They thanked Clamshell Boy as Salmonberry hugged her new brother. "I was to be her dinner tonight," she said. "It was foolish to ignore the elders. Their wisdom is far greater than mine."

Clamshell Boy led the children home, where there was much rejoicing. The People held a celebration of potlatch where they feasted and danced and sang. Everyone exchanged gifts, and told tribal stories.

It is in this way that the Makah still observe their important occasions. It was Clamshell Boy who brought potlatch to the People of the Cape.

THE MAKAH

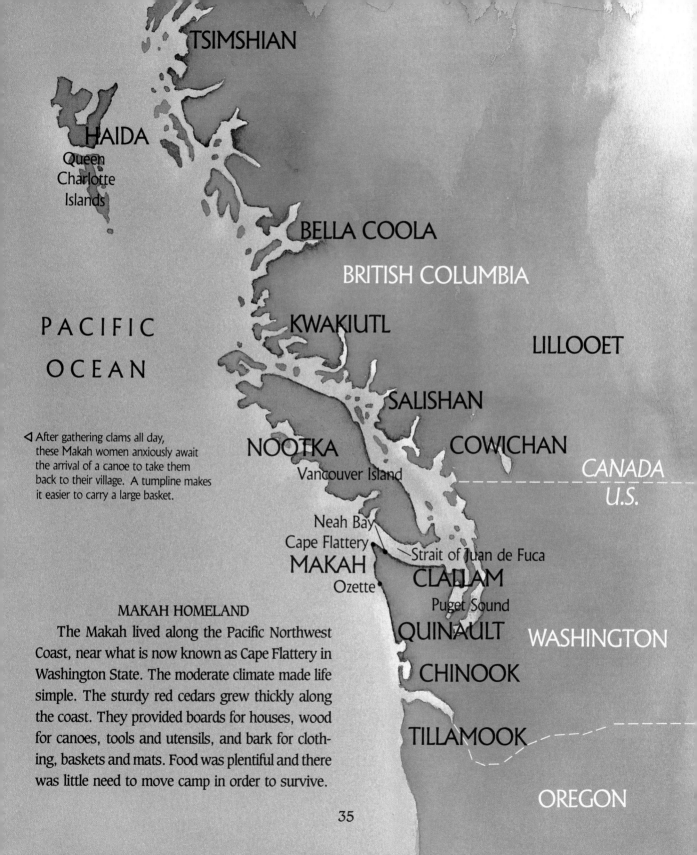

TSIMSHIAN

HAIDA
Queen
Charlotte
Islands

BELLA COOLA

BRITISH COLUMBIA

PACIFIC

OCEAN

KWAKIUTL

LILLOOET

SALISHAN

◁ After gathering clams all day,
these Makah women anxiously await
the arrival of a canoe to take them
back to their village. A tumpline makes
it easier to carry a large basket.

NOOTKA

COWICHAN

CANADA

Vancouver Island

U.S.

Neah Bay
Cape Flattery

Strait of Juan de Fuca

MAKAH
Ozette

CLALLAM

Puget Sound

MAKAH HOMELAND

QUINAULT

WASHINGTON

The Makah lived along the Pacific Northwest
Coast, near what is now known as Cape Flattery in
Washington State. The moderate climate made life
simple. The sturdy red cedars grew thickly along
the coast. They provided boards for houses, wood
for canoes, tools and utensils, and bark for clothing, baskets and mats. Food was plentiful and there
was little need to move camp in order to survive.

CHINOOK

TILLAMOOK

OREGON

35

THE MAKAH

They called themselves "Kweedishchaaht," meaning, "People of the Cape".

Everyone in the village had responsibilities. The men fished, hunted, and warred. They were especially skilled at whaling and were one of the few people who hunted whales at sea.

They were exceptional craftsmen. They made tools such as adzes, drills, wedges, chisels and knives. With these, they cut planks for houses, fashioned canoes, and made bentwood boxes, weaving looms, ceremonial masks, and weapons.

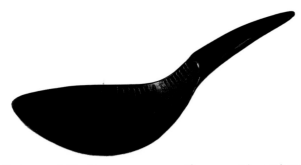

Eating utensils like this spoon were carved from mountain goat horn.

When making a canoe, a man would ask the tree not to hurt him. He would explain that the canoe would be a thing of beauty. Then the log would be hollowed out by burning and carving.

The women tended the children, made clothing, wove baskets, cared for the fish nets and raised their woolly dogs. They gathered shellfish, berries and roots, and preserved the food by salting or sun drying. They boiled food in baskets or wooden bentwood boxes by dropping in heated stones.

The children helped their mothers and learned from their elders what they would need in their adult years. They often improved their skills through games or sports.

Food and shelter were rarely a problem for the Makah, so they had time for socializing. They traded with neighboring villages and occasionally gathered together for a potlatch. This was the Makah way of celebrating important events like birth, death, coming of age, or giving someone a new name.

The person hosting the potlatch, which could last for days, gave away as many gifts to his guests as he could, signifying his wealth. These ceremonies were elaborate and an excellent opportunity for the singing, dancing, and story-telling the people loved. This was particularly true in the winter when the Makah believed the spirits were closest to the villages.

Slavery was a fact of life, too. Slaves were a sign of wealth, which was very important to the Makah. Children were often warned to stay close to camp for fear they'd be stolen by unfriendly tribes. At the same time, the Makah sent war parties out to capture slaves from their enemies, provoking feuds.

This rattle, carved in the shape of a grouse, is typical of rattles used in the Winter Ceremonial, the Klookwalli.

◁ The Wild Man of the Woods was a character in many Makah dances.

SILVER SALMON

MAKAH VILLAGE

Villages consisted of three to twenty communal longhouses lining the beaches. They often housed up to twenty families each. The buildings were made of wooden planks held in place horizontally by pegs. These planks were valuable and difficult to make, so they were portable, in case the village moved to follow a spring salmon run.

The houses had earthen floors and were divided by woven mats into family units, each about the size of a barn stall. Sleeping platforms lined the walls and were padded with moss, cedar bark, or mats woven of cedar or cattails. Each family had its own fire, and a shared cookfire burned in the center of the building, its smoke escaping through a hole in the roof.

SALMONBERRY

FUR SEAL

SALAL

This village of cedar-plank longhouses and large frames for drying salmon was painted by the artist John Webber, who sailed with Captain James Cook in the 1770s.

The Makah Wolf Ritual was an important coming-of-age ceremony.

MAKAH CLOTHING

Because of the mild climate, the Makah often went nude or wore very little clothing. This was true even in the winter, because they spent most of their time indoors where it was warm and dry.

◁ Nose rings were popular among Makah women.
This young woman's earrings were made of cedar bark.

◁ Cedar mats found many uses in the longhouse.

Their clothing consisted of woven capes, skirts, and cone-shaped hats. These were made of cedar which had been soaked and pounded soft. Sometimes feathers, cattail fluff, or fur from specially raised dogs were woven into the cedar fabric. Occasionally, they made garments from animal hides. The Makah rarely used footgear.

41

IMPORTANT DATES

1492	Columbus discovers the New World	**1778**	Captain Cook explores Pacific Northwest Coast
1592	Debatable voyage of Juan de Fuca. He claimed to have discovered the strait bearing his name	**1790**	Nootka Sound Treaty between Britain and Spain gives each the right to trade in the Pacific Northwest
1776	United States declares independence from Britain	**1792**	Captain George Vancouver explores Puget Sound

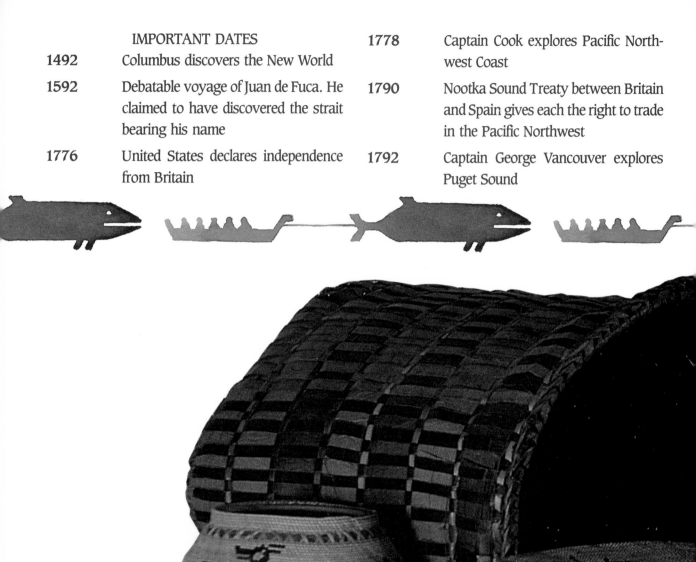

1803-06	Lewis and Clark Expedition opens area to Americans	1936	Makah accept Indian Reorganization Act and a tribal constitution is approved
1853	Washington Territory is created	1970-81	Archeological excavation of Ozette uncovers over 55,000 artifacts and brings a cultural renaissance to Neah Bay
1855	Treaty of Neah Bay is signed		
1913	The last Makah whale hunt takes place		

The Makah were gifted basketmakers. Working in cedar and various grasses, they made baskets both useful and beautiful.

Whalers wore sturdy cedar hats to protect them from the rain.

Makah: Meaning, ''People of the Cape''

Longhouse: Communal dwelling made of cedar planks

Potlatch: Meaning, ''Indian Business'', or ''Giving''

Shaman: Spiritual leader. A powerful person wise in the ways of the spirits as well as in medicine

Sparkling Moon: Approximately the month of March, so named for being crisp and clear

Tumpline: A strap worn across the forehead for carrying baskets on the back

GLOSSARY

Adze: ''D'' shaped carving tool with a blade of bone, tooth, shell, or sometimes metal

Bentwood Box: Box made of wood which was steamed and bent. It was decorated and used for cooking or storage

This whaling model was made about 1893. It shows the harpooner about to strike the whale. The other men stand ready with a second lance and the four sealskin floats used to slow the whale. The carved whale, however, is smaller than actual size. Many whales brought in were much larger than the whaling canoe.

This Makah whaler carries two sealskin floats as well as his large harpoon. The floats were attached to the harpoon point and kept the whale from diving.

PHOTO CREDITS

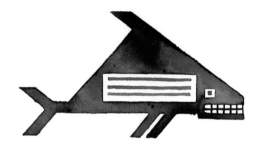

DATE			